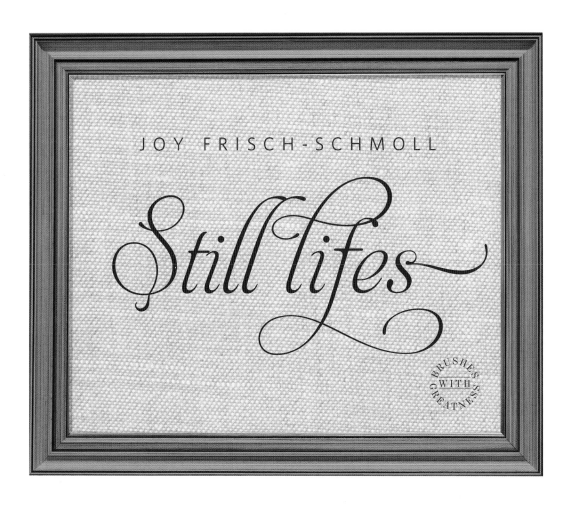

JOY FRISCH-SCHMOLL

Still lifes

BRUSHES WITH GREATNESS

CREATIVE ● EDUCATION

Published by Creative Education P.O. Box 227, Mankato, Minnesota 56002
Creative Education is an imprint of The Creative Company www.thecreativecompany.us

Design and production by Liddy Walseth Art direction by Rita Marshall
Printed in the United States of America

Photographs by Alamy (INTERFOTO, Masterpics), Art Resource (The Metropolitan Museum of Art), The
Bridgeman Art Library (Fitzwilliam Museum, University of Cambridge, UK, Musee des Beaux-Arts, Marseille,
France, The Phillips Collection, Washington, D.C., USA/DACS), Corbis (Alfredo Dagli Orti/The Art Archive, Alinari
Archives, Burstein Collection, Christie's Images, Francis G. Mayer, Massimo Listri, The Andy Warhol Foundation),
Getty Images (Alinari, Jean-Baptiste Simeon Chardin, Dorling Kindersley, French, JGI, SuperStock), iStockphoto
(binabina, ChrisAt, Deanna Finn, Erik Lam, iodrakon, Konstantin Kirillov, Angela Sorrentino), Shutterstock
(501room, Chris Pole, Jakub Krechowicz, optimarc, shooarts), SuperStock (Bridgeman Art Library, Image Asset
Management Ltd.), Wikipedia (Vincent Steenberg)

Library of Congress Cataloging-in-Publication Data
Frisch, Joy.
Still lifes / by Joy Frisch-Schmoll.
p. cm. — (Brushes with greatness)
Includes bibliographical references and index.
Summary: A survey of the painting genre that focuses on carefully arranged inanimate objects, examining the genre's
origins and introducing its notable artists, works, and styles throughout history.
ISBN 978-1-60818-203-9
1. Still-life painting. I. Title.
ND1390.F76 2012
758'.4—dc23   2011040489

First edition

2 4 6 8 9 7 5 3 1

COVER: *STILL LIFE WITH A BASKET*
(C. 1890-95), BY PAUL CÉZANNE
PAGE 2: *UNTITLED,* BY JUAN GRIS

TABLE OF CONTENTS

the Start of Still life

A PAINTING OF A VASE OF FLOWERS OR A BOWL OF FRUIT MAY BE VIEWED TODAY AS SIMPLY A BEAUTIFUL DEMONSTRATION OF ARTISTIC skill—a pretty picture to hang on a wall. But historically, still lifes have been created not merely as decoration but as a means of conveying moral or religious messages. Centuries ago, still life functioned largely as background detail in larger paintings. Over time, renderings of inanimate objects became prized as art in and of themselves, not to mention as a means of visually recording plant and animal specimens. Around the 16th century, the **genre** of still lifes began to blossom into a legitimate form of art—a form that has stood the test of time and retains its treasured status today.

The art of still life painting dates to ancient times. The Egyptians used still lifes to adorn the tombs in which they buried their pharaohs, or kings. Egyptians believed that the food objects, pottery, and other items they depicted in paint would become real for the deceased ruler in the afterlife. Still lifes have also been found in excavations of the ancient Roman cities of Pompeii and Herculaneum, which were buried during the volcanic eruption of Mount Vesuvius in A.D. 79. One Pompeii painting depicts vases and a glass bowl filled with fruit. Roman painters loved demonstrating their technical skill and

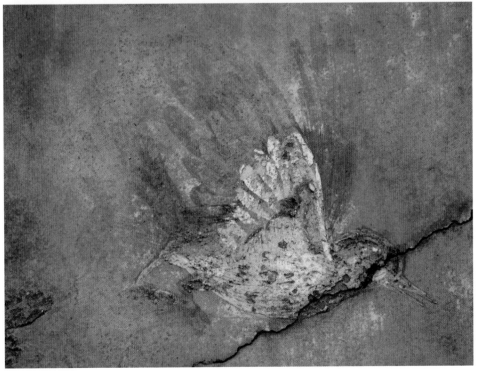

ANCIENT ROMAN ART FOUND IN POMPEII (ABOVE AND LEFT)

created decorative art for the homes of wealthy **patrons**, commonly painting a variety of food items enjoyed by the Roman Empire's richest citizens.

As Christianity's influence spread throughout the **Western** world during the 3rd and 4th centuries a.d., still lifes were featured as background details in many religious paintings. This practice continued during the **Middle Ages**, when most European paintings were made for the Catholic Church. The Church, headquartered in Rome, was at the center of everyday life for many Europeans and played a major role in **commissioning** works of art. Paintings were commonly filled with religious themes intended to encourage Christians to lead lives of piety. Because most people of that time could not read, paintings were powerful reminders of the Bible stories they heard at church, and certain objects were included in these works as a way of adding meaning through **symbolism**. For example, apples were symbolic of sin, as the Bible tells that the first humans— Adam and Eve—defied God by eating this forbidden fruit in the Garden of Eden. Through the Middle Ages and into the **Renaissance**, still life remained primarily a secondary feature in religious paintings.

The invention of oil paint in the early 1400s allowed for new developments in art. Prior to that time, artists had worked primarily with **tempera** paint. Jan van Eyck (c. 1395–1441) and other artists of northern Europe were the first to master the use of oil paint and appreciate its qualities. Unlike tempera, oil paint dried slowly and allowed for the easy mixing of colors, and an artist could alter its consistency to make it either thicker or more fluid. This quality permitted an artist to blend paint by applying it in several thin layers, which allowed for a wide range of visual effects and more realistic depictions of a subject or scene.

As early as 1475, some European artists began to paint still lifes that were **secular** in nature. Italian artist Jacopo de' Barbari (c. 1400–1516) created *Still Life with Partridge, Gauntlets, and Crossbow Bolt* (1504), one of the earliest Renaissance still life paintings to be free of religious content. Other Italians, such as Annibale Carracci (1560–1609), followed suit, soon creating **autonomous** still lifes

STILL LIFE WITH PARTRIDGE, GAUNTLETS, AND CROSSBOW BOLT, BY JACOPO DE' BARBARI

of food, drink, and tableware. Carracci's *The Beaneater* (1590) stands as a notable example of his creations. Still life painting grew in popularity during the 1500s, and a weakening in the power of the Catholic Church contributed to a decline of religious paintings. Northern countries split from Catholicism, and the new Protestant churches did not commission religious artworks—a change that helped allow the still life genre to expand in new directions. Still lifes became particularly popular in Holland and **Flanders**.

Yet even as still life painting grew in popularity and its range of possible subjects expanded, it was often regarded as a lowly form of art on the grounds that—at least in the eyes of many critics— it required only technical skill and no real imagination. Although many prominent portraits and historical paintings contained still life details, many critics thought that the rendering of inanimate objects was not a worthy pursuit on its own. Still life that lacked a biblical association was considered decorative but not "high art," since it was without an intellectual context or moral purpose.

To give their paintings greater moral weight, many still life artists included a variety of symbolic items in their work. Objects were carefully selected to convey a level of meaning above and beyond an attractive physical arrangement. Items such as writing materials, maps, and books suggested knowledge and intellectual curiosity. Certain types of flowers were commonly portrayed as well, both for their distinctive colors and for their rich symbolism. Lilies, for example, represented purity of mind; roses, love; tulips, nobility; and sunflowers, devotion.

Interest in the natural world began to soar in many societies in the 1500s. The Dutch were at the forefront of scientific developments and had a special interest in the observation of the natural world. Items such as shells, insects, exotic fruits, and flowers were collected and traded by the wealthy, and they were prized as objects of study. These items were celebrated in secular still life paintings, created to record these objects and new discoveries such as the tulip, which was brought to Europe from Turkey in the 1500s. Floral still lifes became something of a craze in Europe around 1600, and artists capitalized on the widespread,

newfound interest in nature by producing thousands of still life paintings.

Several distinctive types of still lifes soon emerged, including flower pieces, symbolic pieces, kitchen and market scenes, and breakfast and banquet pieces. Symbolic pieces included any composition with symbolic meaning or story. Among the most popular symbolic pieces were **vanitas**, a classification of works that were often religious in theme and included objects such as skulls, pocket watches, coins, and books. Death and the brevity of life were commonly referenced by wilted flowers, ripened fruit, and snuffed candles. Vanitas served as reminders that the wealth and material possessions accumulated during one's life could not be taken along after death.

Although kitchen and market scenes—which typically showed food and kitchenware along with human figures engaged in activity—lacked religious roots, they, too, were often coded with

THE BEANEATER, BY ANNIBALE CARRACCI

moral lessons. *The Butcher Shop* (1568) by Frenchman Joachim Beuckelaer (1533–74), for example, shows a selection of meats from a common butcher shop in the foreground while simultaneously remarking upon the dangers of drunkenness with the depiction of human figures in the background.

Holland and Flanders in particular emerged as hotbeds for still life art during the Renaissance. Many people of means in those countries had a passion for collecting works of art and curious objects. They loved paintings that were full of hidden meanings and puzzles, and still lifes were the objects of much discussion. Still lifes retained a high level of popularity in Flanders during the 1600s, as the region had a growing and wealthy middle class that produced new patrons who admired and eagerly collected such works. Many merchants sought to decorate their homes with small-scale artwork that reflected their status within society, too. The popularity of secular still life painting soon spread from Holland and Flanders to Germany, Spain, and France.

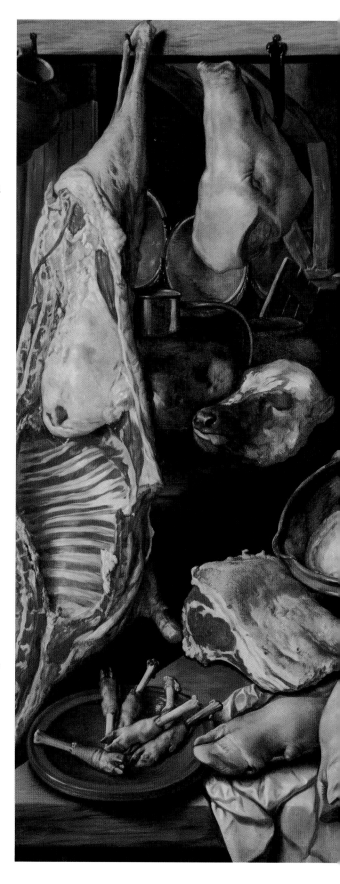

THE BUTCHER SHOP, BY JOACHIM BEUCKELAER

APPRECIATING ART

Young Hare (1502)

Albrecht Dürer, German (1471–1528)

9.9 x 8.9 inches (25.1 x 22.6 cm)

This work by Albrecht Dürer was one of the Western world's first paintings of a pure still life. Prior to this, still life details had been included in many major works of art, but still life did not stand on its own. While other artists were painting grandiose scenes featuring figures from the Bible and ancient mythology, Dürer turned his attention to life around him. Having a great fascination with nature, he made carefully detailed paintings of plants, animals, and birds. It is unknown how Dürer captured the image of the rabbit for this work. He may have sketched the image in the wild and later filled in the details by looking at a dead animal, or he may have caught a rabbit and kept the animal in his studio while he worked.

This detailed **watercolor** shows even the smallest qualities of the rabbit's fur. With meticulous brushstrokes, Dürer depicted the texture of the animal's fur and showed how it lay in different directions. He also used varying hues of brown paint and shading techniques to create the lighter and darker patches of fur. This painting is remarkable not only as a detailed study of the animal but also as a study of light. A warm golden light illuminates the hare from the left. This light, shown on the ears and along the body, adds a spark of life to the eye of the hare. This painting was so well received that several artists followed Dürer's example, creating hare paintings of their own.

From Saints to Flowers

OVER THE COURSE OF HISTORY, MANY ARTISTS HAVE MADE THEIR MARK ON THE STILL LIFE GENRE WITH THE CREATION OF MASTERPIECES AND THE ADVENT OF INFLUENTIAL TECHNIQUES. One of the genre's pioneers was Giotto di Bondone (1266–1377), an Italian painter from Florence. He is widely regarded as the first in a line of great medieval artists who helped give rise to the Renaissance, which originated in Italy.

Giotto is known for creating many large **frescoes** in churches and cathedrals. His masterpiece is the decoration of the Scrovegni Chapel, a church in Padua, Italy, which he completed around 1305. Also known as the Arena Chapel, this work is considered one of the most important masterpieces of Western art. The frescoes focus on the lives of the Virgin Mary and Jesus Christ, and, divided into numerous sections, they show scenes of important events such as Jesus entering the city of Jerusalem before his death. During Giotto's time, paintings were dominated by human figures and religious themes, but Giotto's inclusion of small still life details in his paintings—palms and torches, for instance—enhanced the meaning of the stories they represented.

A WALL OF THE SCROVEGNI CHAPEL

STILL LIFE WITH A JUG OF FLOWERS,
BY HANS MEMLING

Other early religious works included a variety of still life objects. Hans Memling (c. 1433–94), a German-born painter who worked in the Netherlands, created numerous **altarpieces** for churches. In *The Virgin and Child between St. James and St. Dominic* (c. 1490), Memling offers a religious scene in which Mary and the baby Jesus sit on a throne, surrounded by praying saints. An oriental carpet covers the floor beneath them. Such carpets were often integrated into paintings and Christian imagery as symbols of luxury and status. Repeating this symbolism, Memling featured a similar carpet in *Still Life with a Jug of Flowers* (c. 1490), in which a bouquet of flowers sits upon a decorative rug. The flowers, too, are symbolic, as the iris, lily, and columbine flowers were all medieval symbols of the Virgin Mary's joys and sorrows related to Jesus's birth and eventual death.

As still life became more autonomous, artists used the genre to showcase their talents by creating paintings of startling **realism**. Caravaggio (1571–1610), an Italian painter, created dramatic still lifes. As a superb painter of details, Caravaggio laid the foundation for the **Baroque** style of painting, and he was among the earliest of all European artists to create still lifes as a distinct art genre. In addition to frequently including still life elements in his portraits, he created two independent still life paintings of note. The first, *Basket of Fruit* (c. 1599), shows a wicker basket containing a selection of summer fruits, detailed enough to show even the wormholes in the apple. In *Still Life with Fruit on a Stone Ledge* (c. 1601–05), a basket heaped with fruits and vegetables is highlighted by a beam of light. Caravaggio's dramatic use of chiaroscuro, or the technique of contrasting light and shade, soon became a part of many other painters' repertoires.

In addition to depictions of fruit and flowers, animals and raw meats were also commonly shown in still lifes. Flemish painter Frans Snyders (1579–1657), renowned as an animal painter, often included dead animals, particularly killed wild game, in his still lifes. His ability to

depict a wide range of textures such as skin, fur, feathers, glass, and metal was unsurpassed and so phenomenal in its realism that other artists often asked him to paint the animals and birds in their paintings. In his compositions, Snyders sometimes included a hint of action to introduce an element of tension. In *Still Life with Dead Game, Fruits, and Vegetables in a Market* (1614), a young boy picks the pocket of the vendor, while a cat eyes some fighting roosters from beneath the table. In this painting, too, the dead birds and animals displayed at the outdoor market carry their own symbolic meanings. In Snyders's time, the peacock was a symbol of vanity and pride; the wild boar, gluttony; and the deer, purity of heart.

As interest in nature and the collection of natural specimens took hold of art lovers in the 1600s, French painter Jacques Linard (1600–45) created some of his greatest works. *A Still Life with Shells and Coral* (1640) depicts a brightly colored collection of seashells, possessions highly prized at the time. Like many of his contemporaries, Linard worked to create a sensory awareness in

STILL LIFE WITH A RED DEER (1640), BY
FRANS SNYDERS

his compositions by featuring objects that correlated with the different senses. One of his most famous paintings is entitled *The Five Senses and the Four Elements* (1627). Among the objects shown are a bouquet of flowers (smell), a mirror (sight), fruit and a box of sweets (taste), a recorder and a music book (hearing), and playing cards (touch). The materials in the still life also correspond to what were then considered the four elements of the universe: vegetables (earth), a bird flying into the sky (air), a stove (fire), and an iris in a vase (water).

Some still life artists became so popular in the 17th century that they could barely keep up with demand. Dutch Baroque artist Jan Davidsz de Heem (1606–84), for example, did a brisk business with still lifes of wild game, including blood-flecked birds, dying rabbits, and ready-to-eat fish. He also became renowned for lavish banquet pieces that displayed tables full of luxury foods such as tropical fruits, lobsters, and oysters. Such elaborate still lifes of lavish meals were fashionable at that time, as they represented "the good life" of abundance, wealth, and sensory enjoyment. *A Table of Desserts* (1640), de Heem's earliest still life, serves a dual purpose, portraying an impressive banquet of upper-class delicacies while simultaneously reminding its viewers to avoid gluttony. Another de Heem masterpiece, *Vase of Flowers* (1645), shows a multitude of plant species that do not bloom in the same season, displaying the power of an artist to make his own reality by way of arrangements that would not be found naturally.

Another Dutch Baroque artist and a contemporary of de Heem's was Harmen Steenwyck (1612–56). Together with his brother Pieter, Steenwyck studied painting from his uncle, David Bailly, who is often credited with the invention of vanitas. Following his uncle's tradition, Steenwcyk became Europe's foremost painter of vanitas, depicting items that communicated a coded message to the

FLOWERS IN A GLASS VASE (C. 1660, OPPOSITE), BY JAN DAVIDSZ DE HEEM; A DE HEEM SELF-PORTRAIT (ABOVE)

viewer. He painted with incredible realism, as seen in *Still Life with Fruit and Dead Fowl* (1630), in which the translucent grapes look plump enough to pick and the tough texture of the metal is emphasized through the use of highlights and shadows. Steenwcyk is best known for his *Still Life: An Allegory of the Vanities of Human Life* (1640), a vanitas that is essentially a religious work in the form of a still life. The objects shown in this piece were reminders to 17th-century viewers that the wealth and pleasures of this life could become obstacles on the path to eternal salvation.

Throughout much of the history of Western art, female painters commonly chose—or were restricted to painting—still lifes. Like all women of her time, Dutch artist Rachel Ruysch (1664–1750) was forbidden from attending art classes that taught drawing of the nude human form, so she learned to paint flowers instead. This restriction did not limit Ruysch's success, however, because a strong market emerged at that time for floral still lifes. Her compositions typically featured a dark background, meticulous detail, and delicate coloring. *Still Life of Flowers on Woodland Ground* (1690) shows an exotic mix of colorful blooming flowers. To add an element of interest to her paintings, Rysch often included small creatures such as insects, birds, snails, and reptiles, as seen in *Flowers and Insects* (1711). Like certain flower species, insects carried their own particular meanings. Butterflies, for example, represented transformation, dragonflies suggested the passing of time, and ants symbolized hard work.

STILL LIFE WITH FRUIT AND ACORNS (C. 1716), BY RACHEL RUYSCH

APPRECIATING ART

Still Life: An Allegory of the Vanities of Human Life (1640)

Harmen Steenwyck, Dutch (1612–56)

15.4 x 20 inches (39.2 x 50.7 cm)

This famous vanitas painting is filled with references to death and the emptiness of material possessions. It features a skull, a stoneware jar, an empty shell, a watch, a smoking lamp, a Japanese sword, a book, and the bell of a trumpet. A beam of sunlight highlights the central object and focal point, the human skull. The skull—a universal symbol of death—serves as a reminder of mortality. The other items also convey the message that money, power, and knowledge cannot prevent death. The purple silk cloth would have been an item of luxury in the 17th century, as silk was considered the finest of all materials, and purple was the most expensive dye color. The shell, too, was a symbol of worldly wealth and would have been a prized possession. The Japanese samurai sword represents power and implies that not even strength can defeat mortality. The pocket watch marks the length and passing of time. The gold oil lamp has just been extinguished, and a whiff of smoke can be seen, dissolving in the air. And the stoneware jar probably contained water, an element that sustains life.

Steenwyck depicted all the objects with impressive realism. His technique of using small brushstrokes to build up the picture with thin glazes of oil paint allowed him to capture the different textures of the individual items. The sheerness of the silk, the translucence of the bone, and the reflective quality of the steel appear as realistic as the actual surfaces of the objects.

A New Focus in Still Life

BEFORE THE INDUSTRIAL REVOLUTION, WESTERN ART WAS DOMINATED BY A LIMITED NUMBER OF TECHNIQUES IN PAINTING, but during the 1700s and 1800s, major changes in Western society as a whole resulted in changes in art. Groundbreaking developments in manufacturing, transportation, and technology had a profound effect on economies, and more people of the middle class could finally, for the first time, afford to collect art. To keep in step with new societal values and to meet the demands of the growing middle-class market, still life artists began to find new subjects to paint, transitioning from the elegant and regal to the more modest and everyday.

Frenchman Jean-Baptiste-Siméon Chardin (1699–1779) was one 18th-century master who showed that there was great beauty inherent even in humble objects. Instead of depicting objects of luxury, Chardin preferred to portray common domestic items such as bottles, knives, and coffee cups in his still lifes, as in *Glass of Water and Coffee Pot* (1760) and *The Silver Cup* (1769), both of which feature ordinary kitchen items. Chardin's compositions were characterized by simplicity, with objects chosen for their shapes, textures, and colors rather than for any symbolic meaning. Appealing and serene, his paintings were humble in their

THE SILVER CUP, BY JEAN-BAPTISTE-SIMÉON CHARDIN

*VENUS RISING FROM THE SEA—A
DECEPTION*, BY RAPHAELLE PEALE

dimensions, too, usually no larger than one square foot (930 sq cm) in size.

Across the Atlantic Ocean, in the United States, still life painting did not develop as a notable genre until the 18th century. America's first professional painter of still lifes was Raphaelle Peale (1774–1825), who helped found a still life tradition that would remain strong for two centuries. Most of Peale's paintings were small in scale and depicted a few objects arranged on a tabletop in front of a dark background. *Melons and Morning Glories* (1813) shows a split watermelon with juice and seeds spilling onto a table. *Venus Rising from the Sea—A Deception* (1822) shows a different type of composition in which the focal object is a simple white cloth hung on a line. The painting demonstrates Peale's remarkable technical skill, with a realism that lends a lifelike quality to the cloth, showing the fabric's folds and shadows.

The still life tradition soon spread to influence Spanish artists such as Francisco de Goya (1746–1828). Known for his bold techniques and his professed belief that the artist's vision is more important than tradition, Goya is often called "the first of the moderns." Although he was best known for his portraits of Spanish nobility, Goya also painted several still lifes. The objects of his still lifes were often the slabs of meat and piles of fish he saw in the local market. *Still Life, a Butcher's Counter* (1812), for instance, shows the severed head and flanks of a butchered sheep. Goya's art was characterized by bold color, and in this piece, rich shades of red make up the fleshy portions of the raw meat.

Since early times, artists were drawn to still life painting for a variety of reasons. One was that still lifes gave them complete control of the design of their compositions. A painter could choose and arrange his objects in precisely the manner he desired. Robert Chunn, a contemporary American still life artist, reflected upon this advantage of the genre when he said, "Still lifes are always ready to pose. They don't talk or get tired or need to eat. They possess all the qualities of form and color that are needed to keep a painter occupied for the rest of his life."

French artist Paul Cézanne (1839–1906), having lost patience with human subjects who did not sit still while posing, decided to devote himself to still lifes. He painted hundreds of them and came to be widely regarded as history's greatest still life painter. His work was instrumental in the evolution of the genre. Rather than a sole focus on realism, Cézanne concentrated on form, shape, color, and the relationship between objects. In his still lifes, he often arranged a small set of household objects along with fruit and vegetables. *Apples and Oranges* (1899) was one of a series of six compositions featuring the same curtain, pitcher, white fabric, dishes, and fruit. Cézanne's goal as an artist was to create a balanced and pleasing composition with a minimum of detail, and to that end, he often worked so slowly that the fruit would begin to rot before he had finished.

During the 19th century, a new movement developed in France that changed the focus of art even more dramatically. Artist Claude Monet (1840–1926) was the founder of this new style, called Impressionism. Impressionists did not try to hide or smooth their brushstrokes in order to make their still lifes appear real. Their primary concern was the study and depiction of color and light—the attempt to capture an "impression" of objects or scenes in the moment. Impressionists used short, quick dashes of paint, and instead of blending paints on their palettes, they applied pure color to their canvases—a radical change

CLAUDE MONET, PICTURED IN THE EARLY 1900S

from traditional technique. Monet's *Still Life with Anemones* (1885) features bold brushstrokes of bright color to depict flower petals, laid on the canvas in visibly thick strokes.

While Monet and the Impressionists focused on color and light, other artists aimed to create still lifes so lifelike they could trick the viewer. William Harnett (1848–92), an Irish-American painter, practiced a trompe l'oeil ("fool the eye") style of realistic painting. His still lifes of ordinary objects, often arranged on a ledge or hung from a nail, were rendered with such painstaking detail that the paintings could be mistaken for the objects themselves. Popular in America during the late 1800s, "wall-rack pictures" featured objects either tied or attached to

STILL LIFE—VIOLIN AND MUSIC
(1888), BY WILLIAM HARNETT

THE BANANAS, BY
PAUL GAUGUIN

a wall or door. In *The Old Violin* (1886), the background appears to be a door on which the instrument hangs from a nail. When the work was put on public display, many viewers thought that the sheet music and violin were real, with some even reaching out to lift the instrument from its hook.

At the same time in France, Paul Gauguin (1848–1903) spearheaded an artistic movement known as post-Impressionism. Influenced by the Impressionists, Gauguin believed that "colors have their own meanings," and his paintings feature bold use of color, as seen in *Still Life with Fruit and Lemons* (1880), in which bright shades of orange dominate the picture. After becoming dissatisfied with life in France, Gauguin traveled to islands in the South Pacific where he found inspiration in the exotic colors of the land and the vibrant life of the native people. Among the still lifes he created there was *The Bananas* (1891), painted in the first months after he arrived in Tahiti. Gauguin considered it his purpose to simplify form and color in order to create new, personal visions of the world.

Dutch artist Vincent van Gogh (1853–90) shared Gauguin's beliefs in the importance of personal expression and the power of color. Van Gogh used still lifes to express his enjoyment of nature. Birds and their nests were of particular interest to him, as seen in some of his early works, in which they are presented in dark shades of brown and black. After the Dutchman witnessed the bright colors used by the Impressionists in 1880s Paris, his dark and somber palette suddenly lightened. He began painting sunflowers—at first mixed with other flowers, then alone. Over time, van Gogh's paintings of sunflowers and their fiery blooms became his personal emblem. While he often painted somber-colored landscapes, his bright still lifes conveyed cheerfulness. *Four Sunflowers* (1887) and *Lemons, Pears, Apples, Grapes, and an Orange* (1887), created using hundreds of sharp brushstrokes, show uninterrupted yellow, a color van Gogh loved.

APPRECIATING ART

The Ray (1728)

Jean-Baptiste-Siméon Chardin, French (1699–1779)

45.3 x 57.5 inches (114 x 146 cm)

This painting established the reputation of Jean-Baptiste-Siméon Chardin, an artist considered a still life master. Largely self-taught, Chardin was greatly influenced by 17th-century Dutch and Flemish artists. In his paintings, he favored simple yet beautifully textured objects, and his work is characterized by carefully balanced compositions. The treatment of light and texture was of primary concern to Chardin, and he worked methodically to get everything just right, finishing only about four paintings a year. This still life masterpiece is housed in the famous Louvre Museum in Paris, France.

In *The Ray*, the still life arrangement includes a large stingray, oysters, and fish on a tabletop, along with vases and a large white cloth. The startled cat represents a living element that Chardin added to the scene for interest and action. The simplicity of this still life is underscored by the subdued colors and refined, almost grainy textures. Dark and somber tones of brown and black dominate the painting, with the focal point being the stingray, hanging from a large hook. Taking shape in shades of white paint, the ray draws the viewer's eye with tones of pink and red that make up its inner flesh. Chardin's meticulous treatment of light and shadow creates a haunting, almost ghostly face in the underside of the ray, and reflections of light form the round bodies of the vessels and jars on the table. The angled handle of the knife, meanwhile, appears to jut out of the painting.

Modern Art Goes Abstract

BY THE END OF THE 1800S, STILL LIFE WAS WIDELY SEEN AS A RESPECTED PAINTING GENRE, WITH WORKS DECORATING THE WALLS OF HOMES AROUND THE WORLD. The dawn of the 20th century marked the start of a period of increased artistic experimentation. Several significant styles or movements soon emerged, challenging long-established notions within many art genres, including still life.

One of these styles was Fauvism, developed by Frenchman Henri Matisse (1869–1954). Along with other Fauvists (from a French word meaning "wild beasts"), Matisse used outrageous, bold colors in his paintings. Fauvists saw the main function of color as expressing feelings and intensifying the sensory experience of objects such as flowers and fruit, and these painters reduced still life objects to flat shapes filled with vivid hues. They simplified their drawings and exaggerated color for expressive effect, as seen in Matisse's *The Goldfish* (1912). In this work, a bowl of fish takes center stage, and various shapes and colors of leaves and petals fill the rest of the canvas. Matisse wanted his paintings to be celebrations of life, easy to think about and pleasing to view.

Following closely on the heels of Fauvism, the movement known as

THE ACCORDIONIST (1911), BY PABLO PICASSO

Cubism was developed by Spanish artist Pablo Picasso (1881–1973) and his friend Georges Braque (1882–1963) of France. As the first type of modern **abstract** art, Cubism pointed art in an entirely new direction. In their paintings, Cubists reduced objects to simple forms and fragmented them into geometric shapes such as triangles, circles, and cubes. Instead of depicting subjects from one viewpoint or angle, they aimed to capture multiple viewpoints at once. Showing objects as two-dimensional and distorted, Cubists filled canvases with exciting and sometimes baffling patterns. At times, they gave only hints of real-life objects, challenging viewers to study the painting to reach their own interpretations.

Still life was perhaps the most popular genre among Cubists, as it allowed artists to use everyday objects whose forms were still recognizable after they had been simplified and stylized. Picasso's *Mandolin and Guitar* (1924) depicts musical instruments, some of Picasso's favorite objects for still lifes. He kept the minimum information necessary to make the items identifiable: the rounded bodies of the instruments and their lines of strings. Braque's *Violin and Candlestick* (1910) reflects his interest in geometry and perspective while limiting the color palette, offering to the viewer fragmented objects that are barely recognizable.

In the early 1900s, abstract styles became the primary expression of painting in general and came to dominate art in America. In many genres, including still life, abstraction prevailed so completely that it was often hard to identify any subjects or forms within a work of art. In such extreme styles, abstract art was intended not to depict an object so much as to convey a feeling about it. Artists sometimes used nature as a starting point but then transformed it beyond recognition, attempting to provoke a response or emotional reaction within viewers.

Some artists turned otherwise unremarkable still life objects into powerful works of art. Painters such as American artist Georgia O'Keeffe (1887–1986) challenged notions of

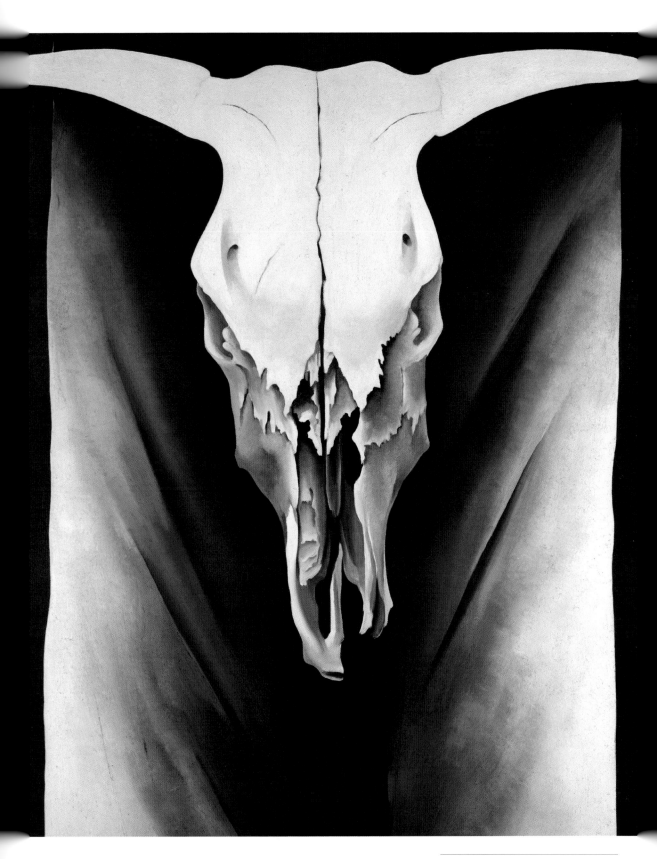

STILL LIFE WITH CHAIR CANING (1912, OPPOSITE), BY PICASSO; *COW'S SKULL: RED, WHITE, AND BLUE* (1931, ABOVE), BY GEORGIA O'KEEFFE

STILL LIFE (NATURAL MORTA) (1953), BY GIORGIO MORANDI

Throughout her long life, she painted hundreds of flower images of many different colors, shapes, and sizes. Her famous *Oriental Poppies* (1928) consists of two giant red poppies that fill a 30- by 40-inch (76.2 x 101.6 cm) canvas.

Originating in the 1920s was Surrealism, a movement that featured elements of surprise along with unexpected **juxtapositions**. Surrealist still lifes were often confusing in their compositions and sometimes humorous in their distortion. They often had a dreamlike quality about them as well. Still lifes by artists such as Spanish painter Salvador Dali (1904–89) are among the most well known of the last century. Dali's works of art ranged from just a little bit strange to shockingly absurd. *Still Life Fast Moving* (1956) shows various objects floating in mid-air. In this painting, Dali perfectly depicted many traditional still life objects, including fruit, tableware, and birds, but the compositional arrangement is unlike that of any previous still life. Dali described the work as illustrating "the decomposition of a fruit dish."

In the mid-1900s, a style called Minimalism emerged to strip art down to its most fundamental features, offering up spare still lifes by such painters as Italian Giorgio Morandi (1890–1964).

modern art. Known for her paintings of flowers, rocks, shells, and animal bones, O'Keeffe transformed her subject matter into large, abstract images. After she saw another artist's still life painting of a flower and felt that it was too small to be fully appreciated, she noted, "I decided if I could paint that flower in a huge scale, you could not ignore its beauty." She began to paint flowers so large that a single flower would fill an entire canvas.

Easily recognizable for their muted colors and quiet simplicity, Morandi's still lifes included a limited selection of ordinary objects. Plain bottles, boxes, jars, jugs, and vases were painted with a dull surface appearance that lacked any reflection or shine. Although the compositions of Morandi's paintings look simple, he often spent weeks adjusting the objects to achieve the placement that would communicate a sense of tranquility. *Still Life with Cups and Boxes* (1951) shows a small collection of objects painted with minimal amounts of detail and shading.

While Morandi and many other still life painters of the 20th century used plain and nondescript objects for their subject matter, other painters chose highly recognizable images as their focus. **Commercial** items recognized for their product labels factored prominently into the Pop Art movement. While most Pop Art paintings were based on still life, the true subject was often the image of a commercial product rather than the physical still life object itself. American artist Andy Warhol (1928–87), a Pop Art pioneer, used his *Campbell's Soup Cans* (1962) to transform the image of an ordinary can of soup into a work of art larger than life. When Warhol first exhibited this work in 1962, each of 32 separate canvases rested on a shelf mounted on the wall, like groceries in a store. Other still lifes by Warhol include *Skull* (1976), a brightly colored, modern version of the traditional vanitas still life.

The first decade of the 21st century made clear that the stylistic options available to still life artists are nearly endless, with a growing number of artists using photography and even computer-generated images to change the nature and definition of still lifes. The evolution of such artistic methods only speaks to the enduring quality of still lifes as a genre, as these paintings continue to find new ways to be expressed and remain relevant. As powerful art forms capable of evoking both reflection and emotion, still life paintings have captivated audiences throughout the centuries. To many artists, such as contemporary American painter Janet Fish, still lifes are a celebration of life. Like the work of many of her peers, past and present, Fish's stunning and brightly colored still lifes seem to say, "Life is good."

ONE HUNDRED CAMPBELL'S SOUP CANS (1962), BY ANDY WARHOL

Campbell's
CONDENSED
BEEF
NOODLE
SOUP

APPRECIATING ART

Vase with Fifteen Sunflowers (1888)

Vincent van Gogh, Dutch (1853–90)

36.2 x 28.7 inches (92.1 x 73 cm)

During the summer of 1888, while he waited for fellow artist Paul Gauguin to arrive for a visit, Vincent van Gogh made a series of five paintings of sunflowers as decorations for his house in France. The paintings were created almost entirely in yellow, a color that signified happiness for van Gogh. Yellow embodied the sunshine of southern France, and the Dutchman—who was vulnerable to bouts of depression—found it to be cheerful. In this painting, sunflowers are shown in various stages, from full bloom to withering. The flowers and petals have been carefully constructed by hundreds of brushstrokes. Van Gogh chose his colors carefully and used them to express his feelings in his art, whether it be happiness or despair, excitement or worry. His expressive technique gives this painting a sort of liveliness that seems to reflect the eagerness van Gogh felt as he waited for his friend's arrival.

This still life was created with a series of quick, short brushstrokes, thickly layered on the canvas. Applying paint with a loaded brush, van Gogh created petals that have a bold effect, and the varying shades of yellow are as vibrant as the brushwork. In the late 1800s, this painting was considered innovative for the range of yellow shown, as newly invented pigments had made wider color arrays possible. Known for working at a brisk pace, van Gogh often completed a painting in a single day. It is quite probable that he finished this work and had it hung on a wall well before Gauguin arrived.

Glossary

abstract—relating to art that does not seek to represent an object or scene but focuses instead on form and design, often with no recognizable content

altarpieces—artwork, such as paintings or sculptures, that is placed above and behind the altar in a church

autonomous—independent or able to stand alone

Baroque—a 17th-century artistic style characterized by drama, tension, and emotional extremes; Baroque paintings often feature deep colors and contrasting shades of light and darkness

commercial—relating to commerce, or the public buying and selling of goods

commissioning—placing an order for a specific work of art

Flanders—a region in northwestern Europe that includes parts of present-day Belgium, France, and the Netherlands

frescoes—paintings made on walls using watercolors on wet plaster

genre—a category in which an artistic work can be classified on the basis of style, technique, or subject matter

juxtapositions—arrangements of two objects placed side by side for the sake of comparison or the creation of contrast

Middle Ages—a period of European history from the 5th century to the 15th century, also known as medieval times

patrons—people who support artists by commissioning and buying artistic works

realism—the quality of depicting people and objects in a true-to-life and unidealized way; capitalized, the term describes such a painting style that arose in France in the mid-19th century

Renaissance—a period of revived interest in classical art, literature, and learning in western Europe from the 1300s to 1500s; the word means "rebirth"

secular—not having to do with religion

symbolism—the practice of using objects that stand for something else, often an abstract idea, such as love or purity

tempera—a type of paint created by mixing pigments with water and egg yolk or other substances

vanitas—still life paintings in which objects symbolize human mortality; the term originates in the Latin word for "vanity" or "emptiness"

watercolor—a painting or style of painting in which pigment is dissolved in water before being applied to the canvas

Western—coming from or having to do with the part of the world that includes Europe and North and South America, where culture has been influenced by ancient Greek and Roman civilizations, as well as Christianity

Selected Bibliography

Art: Over 2,500 Works from Cave to Contemporary. New York: DK Publishing, 2008.

Bernard, Bruce. *Van Gogh*. New York: Dorling Kindersley, 1992.

Chase, Alice Elizabeth. *Famous Artists of the Past: Great Masters and Their Masterpieces*. Edison, N.J.: Chartwell Books, 2004.

Cumming, Robert. *Art Explained*. New York: DK Publishing, 2007.

Janson, H. W., and Anthony F. Janson. *History of Art*. 6th ed. New York: Abrams, 2001.

Koster, Thomas. *50 Artists You Should Know*. New York: Prestel, 2006.

Richardson, Joy. *Looking at Pictures: An Introduction to Art for Young People*. New York: Abrams, 1997.

Thuillier, Jacques. *History of Art*. Paris: Flammarion, 2002.

Most of the paintings referenced in this book can be viewed online. By running an Internet image search using the names of paintings and artists, many works can be quickly located and viewed at the Web sites of various museums and online art galleries.

Index